I0697580

Monetize Your Creativity: Unlocking Revenue Streams for YouTube Creators

Introduction

In the realm of online content creation, YouTube stands as a behemoth, offering creators a platform to share their passions, skills, and creativity with a global audience. However, beyond its role as a mere medium for entertainment or information, YouTube has evolved into a lucrative avenue for individuals to generate substantial income. This Comprehensive Guide delves into the intricacies of monetizing content on this platform, offering aspiring creators a comprehensive roadmap to financial success.

At the heart of YouTube's monetization strategy lies the YouTube Partner Program, a gateway through which creators can access various revenue streams. By enabling monetization, creators open the floodgates to earning revenue from advertisements displayed alongside their videos. This fundamental aspect of YouTube's monetization model serves as the backbone of many creators' income streams, providing a steady flow of revenue based on viewership and engagement. Beyond traditional advertising revenue, creators can explore a multitude of alternative avenues to bolster their earnings. From affiliate marketing, where creators earn commissions by promoting products or services, to sponsored content and product placements, collaborations with brands offer lucrative opportunities to monetize content. Moreover, merchandise sales, crowdfunding platforms like Patreon, and direct viewer contributions through features like Super Chat during live streams further augment creators' earning potential

This guide doesn't just scratch the surface; it delves into the nuances of each monetization method, offering practical insights, tips, and strategies to maximise revenue and build a sustainable income from YouTube content. By understanding and leveraging these diverse monetization avenues, creators can transform their passion into a profitable venture, turning their YouTube channels into thriving businesses in their own right. Whether you're a seasoned creator looking to boost your earnings or a newcomer seeking to monetize your content from the outset, this guide equips you with the knowledge and tools to navigate the ever-evolving landscape of YouTube monetization successfully.

Index

- **Monetize Your Content:** Begin by enabling monetization on your YouTube channel through the YouTube Partner Program.
- **Adsense Revenue:** Earn revenue from ads displayed on your videos by linking your AdSense account to your YouTube channel.
- **Affiliate Marketing:** Promote products or services in your videos using affiliate links and earn commissions for sales generated.
- **Sponsorships:** Collaborate with brands for sponsored content, where they pay you to feature their products or services in your videos.
- **Merchandise Sales:** Create and sell your own branded merchandise such as clothing, accessories, or digital products to your audience.

- **Crowdfunding:** Utilize platforms like Patreon or Kickstarter to allow your viewers to support you financially on a recurring or project basis
- **Super Chat and Channel Memberships:** Enable Super Chat during live streams and offer channel memberships to provide exclusive perks to your subscribers for a fee.
- **Fan Funding:** Enable the fan funding feature on your YouTube channel, allowing viewers to donate money directly to support your content.
- **YouTube Premium Revenue:** Earn a share of the revenue generated from YouTube Premium subscribers who watch your content without ads.
- **Product Reviews and Sponsored Videos:** Partner with companies to create product reviews or sponsored videos, where you receive compensation for featuring their products.
- **Consulting and Coaching:** Offer consulting services or coaching sessions based on your expertise to your audience for a fee.
- **Live Events and Workshops:** Organize live events, workshops, or meetups where fans can attend in person or virtually for a ticket fee.
- **Sell Digital Products:** Create and sell digital products such as ebooks, courses, or presets related to your niche.
- **Brand Partnerships:** Collaborate with established brands for sponsored content, brand integrations, or endorsements in your videos.

- **License Your Content:** License your videos to media outlets, production companies, or other creators for use in their projects in exchange for licensing fees.

Part 1

Monetize Your Content on YouTube: A Comprehensive Guide: Monetizing your content on YouTube is a pivotal step towards turning your passion into profit. With the vast reach of the platform and its diverse audience, creators have the opportunity to generate substantial income through various monetization avenues. One of the primary methods to kickstart your monetization journey is by enabling monetization on your YouTube channel through the YouTube Partner Program.

Understanding the YouTube Partner Program: The YouTube Partner Program (YPP) serves as the gateway for creators to access monetization features on the platform. To qualify for the YPP, channels must meet specific eligibility criteria set by YouTube. These requirements typically include adhering to the platform's community guidelines and copyright policies, as well as reaching a minimum threshold of 1,000 subscribers and 4,000 watch hours within the past 12 months.

Enabling Monetization: Once your channel meets the eligibility criteria, you can proceed to enable monetization. This involves navigating to the "Monetization" section of your YouTube Studio dashboard and following the prompts to sign up for the YouTube Partner Program. Upon acceptance into the program, you gain access to a range of monetization features that allow you to earn revenue from your content.

Earning Revenue from Ads: One of the primary ways creators monetize their content on YouTube is through advertising revenue. By enabling monetization, you grant YouTube permission to display ads on your videos. These ads can take various forms, including pre-roll ads that play before your video, mid-roll ads inserted during longer videos, and display ads that appear alongside your video player.

Types of Ads: Advertisers bid to have their ads displayed on YouTube, and creators earn revenue based on factors such as ad format, viewer engagement, and ad placement. The amount you earn from ads varies depending on factors such as your niche, audience demographics, and the level of advertiser demand for your content.

Monetization Policies and Guidelines: While enabling monetization opens the door to earning revenue from ads, it's essential to adhere to YouTube's monetization policies and guidelines. Violations of these policies, such as click fraud, deceptive practices, or inappropriate content, can result in demonetization or other penalties.

Optimizing Ad Revenue: To maximize ad revenue, creators can optimize their content for monetization by creating engaging videos that attract a broad audience and encourage longer watch times. Additionally, understanding your audience demographics and preferences can help tailor your content to attract high-value advertisers.

Diversifying Your Revenue Streams: While advertising revenue is a significant component of YouTube monetization, creators can also explore additional revenue streams to diversify their income. These may include affiliate marketing, sponsored content, merchandise sales, memberships, and crowdfunding.

Conclusion: Enabling monetization through the YouTube Partner Program is a crucial first step towards monetizing your content on YouTube. By meeting the eligibility criteria and following YouTube's monetization policies, creators can unlock a range of revenue opportunities and turn their passion for creating content into a sustainable income stream. With dedication, creativity, and strategic planning, creators can leverage the power of YouTube to achieve their financial goals and build successful careers in the digital landscape.

Part 2

Maximising AdSense Revenue on YouTube: A Comprehensive Guide : Monetizing your YouTube channel through AdSense is a fundamental strategy for creators looking to turn their passion into profit. By linking your AdSense account to your YouTube channel, you gain access to a lucrative revenue stream derived from ads displayed alongside your videos. Understanding the intricacies of AdSense revenue and implementing effective strategies can significantly enhance your earning potential on the platform.

Linking Your AdSense Account to YouTube: The first step towards earning AdSense revenue on YouTube is to link your AdSense account to your channel. This process involves navigating to the "Monetization" section of your YouTube Studio dashboard and following the prompts to associate your AdSense account with your channel. Once linked, YouTube will display ads on your videos, and you'll start earning revenue based on factors such as ad impressions, clicks, and viewer engagement.

Types of Ads on YouTube: YouTube offers various ad formats that creators can leverage to monetize their content. These include:

1. **Pre-roll Ads:** These ads play before your video starts and are skippable after a few seconds. Creators earn revenue when viewers watch the ad or engage with it in some way.
2. **Mid-roll Ads:** Inserted during longer videos, mid-roll ads provide creators with additional

opportunities to earn revenue. Viewers can encounter these ads at natural breaks within the video content.

3. **Display Ads:** These ads appear alongside the video player or within the recommended videos section. While they may be less intrusive than pre-roll or mid-roll ads, they still contribute to creators' overall AdSense revenue.

Factors Affecting Ad Revenue: Several factors influence the amount of AdSense revenue creators earn from their videos:

1. **Ad Format and Placement:** The type and placement of ads within your videos can impact viewer engagement and, consequently, your ad revenue. Experimenting with different ad formats and placements can help optimize revenue.

2. **Video Content and Audience Engagement** : Engaging content that resonates with your audience can lead to higher viewer retention and increased ad revenue. Understanding your audience's preferences and creating content that keeps them engaged is key to maximizing revenue. Certainly! Here are some examples of audience engagement strategies for a YouTube channel:

   - **Encourage comments:** Prompt viewers to leave comments by asking questions, soliciting feedback, or inviting them to share their thoughts on the video content.

   - **Respond to comments:** Engage with your audience by responding to comments on your videos. This shows that you value their input and encourages further interaction.

   - **Host Q&A sessions:** Dedicate videos specifically to answering questions from your audience. You can gather questions from comments or social media and address them in a dedicated Q&A video.

- **Conduct polls:** Use YouTube's polling feature or ask viewers to vote in the comments on topics related to your content, upcoming videos, or other relevant subjects.
- **Create interactive content:** Design videos that require viewer participation, such as challenges, quizzes, or interactive games where viewers can participate and respond in the comments.
- **Live streams:** Host live streaming sessions where you can directly interact with your audience in real-time, answer questions, and engage in discussions.
- **Community tab:** Utilize YouTube's Community tab to share updates, behind-the-scenes content, polls, and exclusive content with your subscribers.
- **Collaborations:** Collaborate with other creators or invite guest speakers to your channel to introduce new perspectives and engage with their audience as well.
- **Contests and giveaways:** Hold contests or giveaways where viewers can participate by leaving comments, sharing the video, or completing other actions to win prizes.
- **Engage on social media:** Share your YouTube videos on other social media platforms and engage with your audience across multiple channels to increase visibility and foster a sense of community.
- By implementing these audience engagement strategies, you can cultivate a more active and involved community around your YouTube channel, leading to increased

viewership, loyalty, and interaction with your content.

3. **Viewer Demographics and Geographic Location:** Advertisers may pay more to target specific demographics or geographic regions. Creators with audiences that align with advertisers' target demographics may earn higher ad rates.

4. **Advertiser Demand and Seasonality:** Ad rates can fluctuate based on advertiser demand and seasonality. Advertisers may be willing to pay more for ad placements during peak seasons or for high-demand products or services.

Optimizing AdSense Revenue: To maximize AdSense revenue on YouTube, creators can employ various strategies:

1. **Create High-Quality Content:** Producing engaging, high-quality videos that captivate your audience can increase ad views and clicks, leading to higher revenue.

2. **Focus on Audience Retention:** Encourage viewers to watch your videos for longer durations by creating compelling content that maintains their interest throughout.

3. **Experiment with Ad Formats and Placements:** Test different ad formats and placements to determine which ones generate the highest revenue without compromising the viewer experience.

4. **Promote Your Videos:** Increasing visibility and reach for your videos can attract more viewers and, consequently, more ad revenue. Utilizing social media, SEO strategies, and collaborations drive traffic to your channel.

5. **Engage with Your Audience:** Building a strong rapport with your audience can lead to increased

viewer loyalty and engagement, translating into higher ad revenue over time.

Conclusion: Earning AdSense revenue on YouTube is a viable way for creators to monetize their content and generate income from their passion. By linking their AdSense account to their YouTube channel and implementing effective strategies to optimize ad revenue, creators can unlock the full potential of their content and build sustainable revenue streams on the platform. With dedication, creativity, and strategic planning, creators can harness the power of AdSense to achieve their financial goals and establish successful careers in the digital landscape.

Part 3

Unlocking Revenue Potential with Affiliate Marketing on YouTube: Affiliate marketing stands as a dynamic strategy for creators to monetize their YouTube content by promoting products or services and earning commissions for sales generated through affiliate links. This method not only offers a lucrative revenue stream but also provides creators with opportunities to align their content with products relevant to their audience's interests. Understanding the fundamentals of affiliate marketing and implementing effective strategies can empower creators to leverage this model successfully and maximize their earning potential on the platform.

Understanding Affiliate Marketing: At its core, affiliate marketing involves partnering with companies or brands as an affiliate to promote their products or services to your audience. As an affiliate, you earn a commission for each sale or action generated through your unique affiliate links. These links contain tracking codes that allow companies to attribute sales back to your referrals, enabling you to earn commissions for driving conversions.

Implementing Affiliate Marketing on YouTube: To incorporate affiliate marketing into your YouTube strategy, creators can seamlessly integrate affiliate links into their video content. Whether through product reviews, tutorials, or recommendations, creators can strategically showcase affiliate products or services that align with their audience's interests and needs. By transparently disclosing their affiliate partnerships, creators can maintain trust and authenticity with their audience while monetizing their content effectively.

Selecting Affiliate Programs and Partnerships: Choosing the right affiliate programs and partnerships is crucial to the success of your affiliate marketing efforts. Consider factors such as the relevance of the products or services to your niche, the commission rates offered, and the reputation and reliability of the affiliate program or company. Researching and vetting potential affiliate partners ensures that you promote products or services that resonate with your audience and align with your brand values.

Creating Compelling Content: Crafting engaging and informative content is key to driving conversions through affiliate marketing. Whether through product demonstrations, in-depth reviews, or personal endorsements, creators can showcase affiliate products in a way that resonates with their audience and inspires action. Highlighting the benefits, features, and value propositions of the products or services can compel viewers to click on your affiliate links and make a purchase.

Certainly! Here are some popular affiliate programs across various industries:

- **Amazon Associates:** Amazon's affiliate program allows you to earn commissions by promoting products sold on Amazon through affiliate links.

- **ShareASale:** ShareASale is an affiliate marketing network that connects merchants with affiliates, offering a wide range of products and services to promote.
- **Commission Junction (CJ Affiliate):** CJ Affiliate is another affiliate marketing network with a diverse range of advertisers and products to promote, including major brands and retailers.
- **Rakuten Marketing:** Rakuten Marketing offers affiliate marketing opportunities with a variety of merchants across different industries, including fashion, electronics, and more.
- **ClickBank:** ClickBank is a popular affiliate marketplace that specializes in digital products, such as e-books, courses, and software.
- **eBay Partner Network:** eBay's affiliate program allows you to earn commissions by promoting products listed for sale on the eBay platform.
- **Shopify Affiliate Program:** Shopify's affiliate program lets you earn commissions by referring merchants to sign up for Shopify's ecommerce platform.
- **Bluehost Affiliate Program:** Bluehost offers a web hosting affiliate program, allowing you to earn commissions by referring customers to sign up for their hosting services.
- **TripAdvisor Affiliate Program:** TripAdvisor's affiliate program lets you earn commissions by promoting hotel bookings, flights, and other travel-related services through their platform.
- **Awin:** Awin is a global affiliate marketing network that connects publishers with advertisers across various industries, offering a wide range of products and services to promote.

These are just a few examples of popular affiliate programs available. When choosing an affiliate program, consider factors such as the products or services offered, commission rates, payout terms, and the relevance to your audience and content niche.

Optimizing Affiliate Links and Tracking Performance: Utilizing tracking tools and analytics platforms can provide valuable insights into the performance of your affiliate links and campaigns. Monitoring metrics such as click-through rates, conversion rates, and revenue generated allows creators to assess the effectiveness of their affiliate marketing efforts and make data-driven optimizations. Additionally, employing techniques such as A/B testing and tracking affiliate link placements can help identify the most effective strategies for driving conversions.

Maintaining Transparency and Trust: Transparency is paramount in affiliate marketing to maintain trust and credibility with your audience. Disclose your affiliate partnerships clearly and honestly in your content, and ensure that your recommendations are genuine and based on your own experiences and opinions. Building a reputation as a trustworthy and authentic creator fosters long-term relationships with your audience and enhances the effectiveness of your affiliate marketing endeavours.

Conclusion: Affiliate marketing offers creators a versatile and profitable monetization strategy on YouTube, allowing them to generate income by promoting products or services to their audience. By understanding the fundamentals of affiliate marketing, selecting appropriate affiliate partnerships, creating compelling content, and maintaining transparency and trust with their audience, creators can unlock the full potential of affiliate marketing and build sustainable revenue streams on the platform. With dedication, creativity, and strategic implementation, creators can harness the power of affiliate marketing to achieve their financial goals and establish successful careers in the digital landscape.

Part 4

Harnessing Sponsorships: Elevating Your YouTube Revenue Stream. Sponsorships present a lucrative opportunity for YouTube creators to monetize their content by collaborating with brands and featuring their products or services in their videos. This form of sponsored content not only offers creators a source of income but also enables them to leverage their influence and reach to promote brands to their audience. Understanding the dynamics of sponsorships and implementing effective strategies can empower creators to establish mutually beneficial partnerships and unlock the full potential of sponsored content on YouTube .

Understanding Sponsorships: Sponsorships entail a collaboration between creators and brands, where creators endorse or feature products or services in their videos in exchange for compensation from the sponsoring brand. These partnerships can take various forms, including product placements, sponsored shoutouts, dedicated videos, or integrated brand messaging within the content. By aligning with brands that resonate with their audience and content niche, creators can create authentic and engaging sponsored content that enhances their viewers' experience while generating revenue.

Finding Sponsorship Opportunities: Securing sponsorship opportunities requires proactive outreach and networking with brands relevant to your content niche and audience demographics. Creators can leverage platforms such as influencer marketing agencies, creator marketplaces, or direct outreach to brands to explore potential sponsorship collaborations. Building a strong personal brand, demonstrating engagement and influence metrics, and showcasing past sponsored content collaborations can bolster creators' credibility and attractiveness to potential sponsors.

One popular website for connecting YouTube creators with potential sponsorship opportunities is " **FameBit** " (now known as **https://influencermarketinghub.com/famebit/**). This platform allows creators to browse available sponsorship opportunities from brands and submit proposals for collaboration. Brands can also discover and connect with creators whose content aligns with their marketing objectives. YouTube BrandConnect provides a streamlined platform for negotiating terms, managing campaigns, and facilitating payments, making it a convenient option for creators seeking sponsorship opportunities.

Negotiating Sponsorship Deals: Negotiating sponsorship deals involves establishing mutually beneficial terms and agreements between creators and sponsoring brands. Factors to consider include compensation, deliverables, exclusivity agreements, creative control, and disclosure requirements. By clearly defining expectations, objectives, and deliverables upfront, creators can ensure a smooth and successful partnership with sponsoring brands while safeguarding their creative integrity and authenticity.

Creating Compelling Sponsored Content: Crafting compelling sponsored content is essential to engaging viewers and driving results for sponsoring brands. Creators should seamlessly integrate sponsored messaging into their videos in a way that feels natural and authentic to their content style and audience preferences. Providing value to viewers through informative, entertaining, or educational content while showcasing the sponsored product or service enhances the overall viewer experience and strengthens the brand's message.

Maintaining Transparency and Authenticity:
Maintaining transparency and authenticity is paramount in sponsored content to preserve trust and credibility with your audience. Creators should clearly disclose their sponsorship relationships in compliance with advertising guidelines and regulations. Additionally, ensuring that sponsored recommendations are genuine and based on personal experiences and opinions reinforces trust with viewers and strengthens the effectiveness of sponsored content collaborations.

Measuring and Reporting Performance: Evaluating the performance of sponsored content collaborations involves tracking key metrics such as engagement, reach, conversion rates, and brand sentiment. Providing sponsors with comprehensive performance reports and insights demonstrates the value and impact of the partnership and strengthens future collaboration opportunities. Additionally, soliciting feedback from viewers and sponsors can inform future content strategies and partnership negotiations.

Conclusion: Sponsorships offer YouTube creators a valuable opportunity to monetize their content while collaborating with brands to promote products or services to their audience. By understanding the dynamics of sponsorships, securing relevant partnership opportunities, negotiating mutually beneficial terms, creating compelling sponsored content, and maintaining transparency and authenticity with their audience, creators can harness the power of sponsorships to diversify their revenue streams and build sustainable partnerships in the digital landscape. With creativity, professionalism, and strategic collaboration, creators can unlock the full potential of sponsored content on YouTube and establish successful careers as influential content creators.

Part 5

Elevating Revenue with Merchandise Sales: A Comprehensive Guide for YouTube Creators. Merchandise sales present an enticing opportunity for YouTube creators to monetize their content and engage with their audience on a deeper level. By creating and selling branded merchandise such as clothing, accessories, or digital products, creators can not only diversify their revenue streams but also cultivate a sense of community and identity among their fanbase. Understanding the nuances of merchandise sales and implementing effective strategies can empower creators to leverage this monetization model successfully and build a thriving merchandising business on YouTube.

Creating Branded Merchandise: The first step in harnessing merchandise sales is to conceptualize and design branded products that resonate with your audience and reflect your content niche and brand identity. Whether it's clothing, accessories, or digital products such as ebooks, presets, or artwork, creators should focus on creating high-quality, visually appealing merchandise that aligns with their brand aesthetic and values.

Partnering with Merchandise Platforms: To streamline the merchandising process, creators can partner with third-party merchandise platforms that specialize in producing, fulfilling, and shipping custom merchandise. Platforms such as Teespring, Spreadshirt, or Redbubble offer creators a hassle-free solution for designing, listing, and selling their branded products, eliminating the need for inventory management and order fulfilment.

Promoting Merchandise to Your Audience: Promoting merchandise to your audience involves strategically integrating product promotions into your content and leveraging various marketing channels to drive sales.

Creators can showcase their merchandise in their videos through product placements, shoutouts, or dedicated merch announcement videos. Additionally, promoting merchandise on social media platforms, through email newsletters, or during live streams can expand reach and visibility to potential customers.

Creating Limited Editions and Exclusive Drops: Creating limited edition or exclusive merchandise releases can generate excitement and urgency among your audience, driving sales and fostering a sense of exclusivity and collectibility. By offering limited quantities or exclusive designs, creators can incentivize their audience to make a purchase and create a buzz around their merchandise releases.

Offering Bundles and Special Promotions: To incentivize larger purchases and increase average order value, creators can offer bundled merchandise packages or special promotions such as discounts, freebies, or limited-time offers. Bundling related products or offering exclusive perks to customers who purchase multiple items can encourage impulse buying and drive sales volume.

Engaging with Your Community: Engaging with your community and soliciting feedback can inform your merchandise design and marketing strategies and strengthen your relationship with your audience. Creators can involve their audience in the merchandising process by soliciting design ideas, conducting polls or surveys, and incorporating fan input into their merchandise offerings.

Monitoring Performance and Iterating: Monitoring the performance of your merchandise sales involves tracking key metrics such as sales volume, revenue, conversion rates, and customer feedback. Analyzing this data allows creators to identify trends, evaluate the effectiveness of their merchandising strategies, and iterate on their product offerings to better meet the needs and preferences of their audience.

Conclusion: Merchandise sales offer YouTube creators a versatile and profitable monetization strategy, allowing them to monetize their content while fostering deeper connections with their audience. By creating high-quality, branded merchandise that resonates with their audience, partnering with merchandise platforms, promoting merchandise effectively, and engaging with their community, creators can unlock the full potential of merchandise sales and build a successful merchandising business on YouTube. With creativity, strategic planning, and a focus on audience engagement, creators can leverage merchandise sales to diversify their revenue streams and establish long-term success in the digital landscape.

Part 6

Empowering Financial Support through Crowdfunding: A Comprehensive Overview for YouTube Creators. Crowdfunding platforms such as Patreon and Kickstarter offer YouTube creators a powerful avenue to secure financial support from their audience on either a recurring or project basis. This model not only provides creators with a sustainable source of income but also fosters a sense of community and reciprocity among supporters. Understanding the intricacies of crowdfunding and implementing effective strategies can enable creators to leverage this model successfully and build a dedicated fanbase that is invested in their content and success.

Understanding Crowdfunding Platforms: Crowdfunding platforms like Patreon and Kickstarter serve as intermediaries that facilitate financial support from fans to creators. While Patreon focuses on ongoing, subscription-based support, Kickstarter primarily facilitates one-time pledges for specific projects or initiatives. Both platforms provide creators with tools to showcase their work, engage with supporters, and offer exclusive perks or rewards in exchange for financial contributions.

Setting Up Your Crowdfunding Campaign: Launching a crowdfunding campaign involves creating a compelling pitch or project proposal that resonates with your audience and incentivizes them to support you financially. Creators should articulate their goals, vision, and value proposition clearly, and outline the benefits and rewards supporters will receive in return for their contributions. Whether it's access to exclusive content, behind-the-scenes updates, or personalised interactions, offering tangible rewards can incentivise fans to pledge their support.

Engaging with Your Supporters: Engaging with your supporters is crucial to fostering a sense of community and reciprocity on crowdfunding platforms. Creators should actively communicate with their supporters, express gratitude for their contributions, and provide regular updates on their progress and projects. Hosting Q&A sessions, live streams, or exclusive events for supporters can deepen the connection and foster loyalty among your fanbase.

Offering Exclusive Perks and Rewards: Offering exclusive perks and rewards to supporters can incentivize them to pledge their support and increase their contribution levels. Creators can tailor their reward tiers to cater to different supporter preferences and budgetary constraints, offering a range of benefits such as early access to content, merchandise discounts, exclusive merchandise, personalised shoutouts, or one-on-one interactions.

Promoting Your Crowdfunding Campaign: Promoting your crowdfunding campaign involves leveraging various marketing channels to reach and engage with your audience effectively. Creators can promote their campaign through their YouTube channel, social media platforms, email newsletters, and collaborations with other creators. Utilising compelling visuals, storytelling, and calls to action can capture attention and encourage supporters to pledge their support.

Delivering on Your Promises: Delivering on your promises is essential to maintaining trust and credibility with your supporters. Creators should fulfil their commitments, deliver rewards in a timely manner, and keep supporters informed of any delays or changes to their plans. Transparency and communication are key to building and sustaining a positive relationship with your audience.

Monitoring and Evaluating Your Campaign: Monitoring and evaluating your crowdfunding campaign involves tracking key metrics such as funding progress, supporter engagement, and conversion rates. Analyzing this data allows creators to assess the effectiveness of their campaign strategies, identify areas for improvement, and make informed decisions to optimize their campaign performance.

Conclusion: Crowdfunding offers YouTube creators a powerful mechanism to secure financial support from their audience and cultivate a dedicated community of supporters. By leveraging crowdfunding platforms, engaging with supporters, offering exclusive perks and rewards, promoting their campaign effectively, and delivering on their promises, creators can unlock the full potential of crowdfunding and build a sustainable source of income while pursuing their creative passions. With creativity, authenticity, and a focus on community building, creators can harness the power of crowdfunding to achieve their goals and establish long-term success in the digital landscape.

Part 7

Super Chat and Channel Memberships: Enhancing Viewer Engagement and Monetization on YouTube

Super Chat and Channel Memberships are innovative features offered by YouTube that enable creators to enhance viewer engagement and monetize their content directly from their audience. These features provide creators with additional revenue streams while offering viewers exclusive perks and benefits in return for their support. Understanding the dynamics of Super Chat and Channel Memberships and implementing effective strategies can empower creators to leverage these features successfully and build a thriving community around their content.

Understanding Super Chat: Super Chat allows viewers to purchase highlighted messages that stand out during live chat sessions within a creator's live stream. By paying for a Super Chat, viewers can ensure that their message is prominently displayed and receives special attention from the creator and other viewers. The cost of a Super Chat varies depending on factors such as message duration and the viewer's chosen amount.

Leveraging Super Chat for Monetization: Super Chat provides creators with a direct and immediate way to monetize their live streams and engage with their audience in real-time. Creators can incentivize viewers to purchase Super Chats by offering shoutouts, special acknowledgments, or exclusive interactions during their live streams. Additionally, creators can set minimum purchase amounts or offer tiered incentives to encourage larger Super Chat contributions.

Understanding Channel Memberships: Channel Memberships allow viewers to become paying members of a creator's channel in exchange for exclusive perks and benefits. These perks may include badges, emojis, exclusive content, access to members-only live chats or community posts, and other special privileges. Channel Memberships typically involve a monthly subscription fee, with creators setting the price and determining the perks offered to members.

Fostering Community and Engagement: Channel Memberships foster a sense of belonging and exclusivity among viewers, encouraging them to support their favourite creators financially in exchange for access to premium content and perks. By offering unique and valuable benefits to channel members, creators can cultivate a dedicated community of supporters who feel invested in the success of the channel.

Promoting Channel Memberships: Promoting Channel Memberships involves highlighting the benefits and perks of membership to encourage viewers to join. Creators can promote Channel Memberships through their videos, live streams, community posts, and social media platforms. Offering exclusive previews or behind-the-scenes glimpses of members-only content can entice viewers to become paying members of the channel.

Monetizing Live Streams and Community Engagement: Super Chat and Channel Memberships provide creators with complementary monetization tools that allow them to monetize their live streams and engage with their audience in meaningful ways. By incorporating these features into their content strategy, creators can diversify their revenue streams and build a sustainable income from their YouTube channel while fostering a vibrant and engaged community of supporters.

Conclusion: Super Chat and Channel Memberships offer YouTube creators powerful tools to enhance viewer engagement and monetize their content directly from their audience. By leveraging these features effectively, creators can cultivate a dedicated community of supporters, offer exclusive perks and benefits to their audience, and build a sustainable income stream from their YouTube channel. With creativity, authenticity, and a focus on community building, creators can harness the power of Super Chat and Channel Memberships to achieve their goals and establish long-term success in the digital landscape.

Part 8

Fan Funding: Empowering Direct Support for YouTube Creators: Fan Funding, also known as Fan Donations or Fan Contributions, is a feature offered by YouTube that enables creators to receive direct financial support from their viewers. This feature allows fans to contribute monetary donations to their favourite creators as a gesture of appreciation for their content. Understanding the dynamics of Fan Funding and implementing effective strategies can empower creators to leverage this feature to supplement their income and cultivate a closer connection with their audience.

Enabling Fan Funding: Enabling Fan Funding on a YouTube channel allows creators to receive donations directly from viewers who wish to support their content financially. Creators can activate this feature through their YouTube channel settings, and once enabled, viewers will have the option to make donations during live streams or through designated donation links provided by the creator.

Facilitating Direct Support: Fan Funding provides creators with a direct and immediate way to receive financial support from their audience without the need for intermediaries or third-party platforms. By enabling Fan Funding, creators can encourage viewers who value their content to contribute donations, thereby supplementing their income and allowing them to continue creating content without relying solely on advertising revenue.

Engaging with Supporters: Engaging with supporters who contribute donations through Fan Funding is crucial to fostering a sense of appreciation and connection with the audience. Creators can acknowledge and thank donors during live streams, through personalized messages or shoutouts, or by offering exclusive perks or benefits to donors, such as access to exclusive content or behind-the-scenes updates.

Incentivizing Donations: Incentivizing donations through Fan Funding involves offering tangible or intangible rewards to donors as a token of appreciation for their support. Creators can offer perks such as exclusive badges, emojis, or access to members-only content to donors who contribute above a certain threshold. By providing incentives, creators can encourage viewers to make larger donations and increase their overall contributions.

Promoting Fan Funding: Promoting Fan Funding involves raising awareness of the feature and encouraging viewers to contribute donations to support the creator's content. Creators can promote Fan Funding through their videos, live streams, community posts, social media platforms, and email newsletters. Highlighting the impact of viewer donations and expressing gratitude for the support can incentivize more viewers to contribute.

Transparency and Trust: Maintaining transparency and trust is essential when leveraging Fan Funding to receive donations from viewers. Creators should clearly communicate how donations will be used to support their content creation efforts and provide regular updates on how viewer contributions are making a difference. Building trust with the audience fosters a positive relationship and encourages continued support through Fan Funding.

Conclusion: Fan Funding offers YouTube creators a direct and immediate way to receive financial support from their audience, allowing them to supplement their income and continue creating content without relying solely on advertising revenue. By enabling Fan Funding, engaging with supporters, incentivizing donations, promoting the feature, and maintaining transparency and trust with their audience, creators can harness the power of direct support to build a sustainable income stream and cultivate a closer connection with their fans. With creativity, authenticity, and a focus on community building, creators can leverage Fan Funding to achieve their goals and establish long-term success in the digital landscape.

Part 9

Maximising YouTube Premium Revenue: Leveraging Ad-Free Viewing for YouTube Creators

YouTube Premium Revenue offers creators a unique opportunity to earn a share of revenue from subscribers who enjoy their content without ads. This feature, part of YouTube's subscription service, provides creators with an additional revenue stream based on the watch time of YouTube Premium subscribers. Understanding the dynamics of YouTube Premium Revenue and implementing effective strategies can empower creators to leverage this feature to supplement their income and enhance their overall monetization strategy.

Understanding YouTube Premium: YouTube Premium is a subscription service offered by YouTube that provides users with an ad-free viewing experience, access to exclusive content, and other premium features such as offline playback and background play. Subscribers pay a monthly fee for these benefits, and creators receive a portion of the subscription revenue based on the watch time of their content by YouTube Premium subscribers.

Earning Revenue from YouTube Premium Subscribers: Creators earn revenue from YouTube Premium subscribers who watch their content without ads. YouTube distributes a portion of the subscription revenue to creators based on the watch time of their content by YouTube Premium subscribers. This revenue is calculated and paid out to creators on a monthly basis, alongside other revenue streams such as advertising revenue and channel memberships.

Maximising YouTube Premium Revenue: To maximise YouTube Premium Revenue, creators can focus on creating engaging, high-quality content that appeals to YouTube Premium subscribers. Since YouTube Premium subscribers watch content without ads, creators can prioritize content formats that encourage longer watch times, such as longer-form videos, series, or playlists. By optimising for watch time and engagement, creators can increase their share of YouTube Premium Revenue.

Promoting YouTube Premium Subscriptions: Encouraging viewers to subscribe to YouTube Premium can indirectly benefit creators by increasing their potential revenue from YouTube Premium subscribers. Creators can promote the benefits of YouTube Premium, such as ad-free viewing, access to exclusive content, and offline playback, to their audience through their videos, community posts, and social media platforms. Offering exclusive perks or incentives to viewers who subscribe to YouTube Premium can further incentivise subscriptions.

Analysing Performance and Optimising Strategy: Monitoring the performance of content among YouTube Premium subscribers can provide valuable insights into viewer preferences and behaviour. Creators can analyse metrics such as watch time, audience retention, and engagement to identify trends and patterns among

YouTube Premium subscribers. By leveraging this data, creators can tailor their content strategy to better cater to the preferences of YouTube Premium subscribers and maximise their YouTube Premium Revenue.

Conclusion: YouTube Premium Revenue offers creators a valuable revenue stream based on the watch time of YouTube Premium subscribers. By understanding the dynamics of YouTube Premium Revenue, creating engaging content that appeals to YouTube Premium subscribers, promoting YouTube Premium subscriptions to their audience, and analysing performance to optimise their strategy, creators can leverage this feature to supplement their income and enhance their overall monetisation strategy on YouTube. With creativity, strategic planning, and a focus on audience engagement, creators can maximize their YouTube Premium Revenue and build a sustainable income from their content on the platform.

Part 10

Leveraging Product Reviews and Sponsored Videos: Enhancing Monetization and Collaboration on YouTube

Product Reviews and Sponsored Videos represent valuable opportunities for YouTube creators to collaborate with companies and monetize their content by featuring products or services in their videos. These partnerships provide creators with compensation in exchange for showcasing and promoting brands' offerings to their audience. Understanding the dynamics of product reviews and sponsored videos and implementing effective strategies can empower creators to leverage these collaborations to enhance their monetization efforts and build mutually beneficial relationships with brands.

Product Reviews: Product reviews involve creators testing and evaluating products or services and sharing their honest opinions and experiences with their audience. These reviews provide valuable insights and recommendations to viewers who may be considering purchasing the featured products. Creators can leverage their expertise and credibility to provide authentic and unbiased reviews that resonate with their audience and foster trust and credibility with viewers.

Sponsored Videos: Sponsored videos entail creators partnering with companies to feature their products or services in their content in exchange for compensation. These collaborations can take various forms, including dedicated product showcases, tutorials, endorsements, or integrations within the creator's videos. By aligning with brands that resonate with their audience and content niche, creators can create sponsored videos that seamlessly integrate brand messaging while providing value to their viewers.

Benefits of Product Reviews and Sponsored Videos: Product reviews and sponsored videos offer several benefits to both creators and brands. For creators, these collaborations provide an additional source of revenue and allow them to monetize their content while providing valuable information and entertainment to their audience. For brands, partnering with creators allows them to reach a targeted and engaged audience, build brand awareness, and drive sales through authentic and trusted endorsements.

Building Mutually Beneficial Relationships: Successful product reviews and sponsored videos are built on trust, transparency, and mutual respect between creators and brands. Creators should prioritize partnering with brands whose values align with their own and whose products or services genuinely resonate with their audience. By fostering open communication, setting clear expectations, and delivering on promises, creators can build long-term, mutually beneficial relationships with brands that result in repeat collaborations and sustained revenue opportunities.

Maintaining Authenticity and Credibility: Maintaining authenticity and credibility is crucial when creating product reviews and sponsored videos to preserve trust and credibility with your audience. Creators should disclose their sponsorship relationships transparently and ensure that their reviews and endorsements are honest, unbiased, and based on their genuine experiences with the featured products or services. Building a reputation for authenticity strengthens the bond with your audience and enhances the effectiveness of sponsored content collaborations.

Navigating Legal and Ethical Considerations: Navigating legal and ethical considerations is essential when creating product reviews and sponsored videos to ensure compliance with advertising regulations and guidelines. Creators should familiarize themselves with relevant laws and regulations regarding disclosure, endorsements, and sponsored content, such as the Federal Trade Commission (FTC) guidelines in the United States. Failure to comply with these regulations can result in penalties and damage to your reputation as a creator.

Conclusion: Product reviews and sponsored videos offer YouTube creators valuable opportunities to collaborate with brands and monetize their content while providing valuable information and entertainment to their audience. By prioritizing authenticity, transparency, and alignment with their audience's interests, creators can create sponsored content that resonates with viewers and delivers tangible results for brands. With careful planning, effective communication, and a focus on building mutually beneficial relationships, creators can leverage product reviews and sponsored videos to enhance their monetization efforts and establish themselves as trusted influencers in their niche.

Part 11

Monetizing Expertise: Unlocking Revenue Potential through Consulting and Coaching on YouTube
Consulting and Coaching services offer YouTube creators a unique opportunity to monetize their expertise and knowledge by providing personalized advice, guidance, and mentorship to their audience for a fee. By leveraging their expertise in a particular niche or industry, creators can offer valuable insights and support to individuals seeking to improve their skills, achieve their goals, or overcome challenges. Understanding the dynamics of consulting and coaching and implementing effective strategies can empower creators to build a thriving consulting and coaching business and diversify their revenue streams on YouTube.

Offering Consulting Services: Consulting services involve providing expert advice, analysis, and recommendations to individuals or businesses seeking guidance in a specific area of expertise. Creators can offer consulting services in various fields such as business, marketing, finance, health, fitness, education, or personal development, depending on their skills, knowledge, and experience. Consulting engagements may range from one-time sessions to ongoing support and collaboration, tailored to the client's needs and objectives.

Providing Coaching Sessions: Coaching sessions focus on providing personalized support, encouragement, and accountability to individuals seeking to achieve specific goals or make positive changes in their lives. Creators can offer coaching services in areas such as career development, leadership, productivity, mindset, relationships, or wellness, drawing on their expertise and experience to guide and empower their clients towards success. Coaching sessions typically involve regular meetings or sessions conducted remotely or in person.

Monetizing Consulting and Coaching: Creators can monetize their consulting and coaching services by charging clients a fee for their time, expertise, and support. Pricing structures may vary depending on factors such as the duration and complexity of the engagement, the level of expertise required, and the value delivered to the client. Creators can offer individual sessions, package deals, or subscription-based services, depending on their preferences and the needs of their clients.

Promoting Consulting and Coaching Services: Promoting consulting and coaching services involves raising awareness of the services offered and attracting potential clients through marketing and promotion. Creators can promote their consulting and coaching services through their YouTube channel, website, social media platforms, email newsletters, and networking events. Offering free resources, such as webinars, workshops, or downloadable guides, can showcase the creator's expertise and attract clients interested in their services.

Building Credibility and Trust: Building credibility and trust is essential when offering consulting and coaching services to establish yourself as a trusted authority in your niche or industry. Creators should showcase their expertise, credentials, and success stories through testimonials, case studies, or portfolio examples. Providing value, demonstrating results, and delivering exceptional service can foster positive word-of-mouth referrals and repeat business from satisfied clients.

Ensuring Client Success: Ensuring client success is paramount when offering consulting and coaching services to deliver tangible value and results to clients.

Creators should listen actively to clients' needs, goals, and challenges, and tailor their advice and recommendations to address their specific situation and objectives. Providing ongoing support, accountability, and feedback can empower clients to make progress and achieve their goals with confidence.

Conclusion: Consulting and Coaching services offer YouTube creators a valuable opportunity to monetize their expertise and knowledge while providing personalized support and guidance to their audience. By leveraging their skills, experience, and passion in a particular niche or industry, creators can build a thriving consulting and coaching business and empower individuals to achieve their goals and aspirations. With dedication, professionalism, and a focus on delivering value, creators can unlock the full potential of consulting and coaching services and establish themselves as trusted advisors and mentors in their field.

Part 12

Engaging Fans: Hosting Live Events and Workshops for In-Person and Virtual Participation

Live Events and Workshops provide YouTube creators with dynamic opportunities to connect with their audience, share expertise, and monetize their content through ticket sales. Whether held in person or virtually, these events offer fans a unique experience to interact directly with their favourite creators, learn new skills, and engage with like-minded individuals. Understanding the dynamics of hosting live events and workshops and implementing effective strategies can empower creators to build a vibrant community and generate revenue while delivering value to their audience.

Organizing Live Events: Live events, such as meetups, conferences, or performances, allow creators to engage with their audience in person and create memorable experiences. Creators can organise live events in various locations, ranging from local meetups to international tours, depending on their audience reach and logistical considerations. Live events provide fans with the opportunity to meet their favourite creators, attend panels or workshops, participate in Q&A sessions, and interact with other fans.

Hosting Virtual Workshops: Virtual workshops or webinars offer creators the flexibility to reach a global audience and deliver educational or instructional content online. Creators can host virtual workshops on platforms such as Zoom, Google Meet, or YouTube Live, providing attendees with access to live presentations, demonstrations, discussions, and Q&A sessions from the comfort of their own homes. Virtual workshops can cover a wide range of topics, including education, arts and crafts, fitness, cooking, business, or personal development.

Monetizing Live Events and Workshops: Monetizing live events and workshops involves charging attendees a ticket fee for access to the event or workshop experience. Creators can offer different ticket tiers or packages with varying levels of access, perks, and benefits to cater to different audience preferences and budgetary constraints. Ticket prices may vary depending on factors such as the duration, content, location, and exclusivity of the event.

Promoting Live Events and Workshops: Promoting live events and workshops involves raising awareness of the event and attracting attendees through marketing and promotion. Creators can promote their events through their YouTube channel, social media platforms, email newsletters, website, and partnerships with other creators or organisations. Offering early bird discounts, limited-time promotions, or exclusive perks to early registrants can incentivise fans to purchase tickets and secure their spot at the event.

Enhancing Audience Engagement: Enhancing audience engagement is essential to creating a memorable and impactful event experience for attendees. Creators can incorporate interactive elements such as live polls, quizzes, audience participation activities, or networking opportunities to keep attendees engaged and entertained throughout the event. Providing opportunities for fans to interact with the creator and each other fosters a sense of community and connection among attendees.

Ensuring Event Success: Ensuring event success requires careful planning, organisation, and execution to deliver a seamless and enjoyable experience for attendees. Creators should consider factors such as venue selection, event logistics, scheduling, content planning, technical setup, and attendee communication to ensure everything runs smoothly on the day of the event. Collecting feedback from attendees post-event can inform future event planning and improvements.

Conclusion: Live Events and Workshops offer YouTube creators exciting opportunities to engage with their audience, share expertise, and monetize their content through ticket sales. By organising in-person meetups, conferences, or performances, or hosting virtual workshops and webinars, creators can create unique experiences that resonate with their audience and foster a sense of community and connection. With careful planning, effective promotion, and a focus on delivering value and engagement, creators can leverage live events and workshops to build a thriving community and generate revenue while enriching the fan experience.

Part 13

Monetising Creativity: Crafting and Selling Digital Products to Your Niche Audience

Selling digital products, such as ebooks, courses, or presets, presents YouTube creators with an excellent opportunity to monetise their expertise and provide value to their audience in a convenient and accessible format. By leveraging their knowledge and skills within their niche, creators can develop digital products that cater to the specific needs and interests of their audience, while generating revenue streams beyond traditional advertising. Understanding the dynamics of creating and selling digital products, and implementing effective strategies, can empower creators to build a sustainable income while enriching their relationship with their audience.

Creating Digital Products: Digital products encompass a wide range of offerings, including ebooks, online courses, video tutorials, presets, templates, or digital downloads, that creators can develop and sell to their audience. These products leverage the creator's expertise, insights, and unique perspective within their niche to provide valuable information, resources, or tools that address the needs and interests of their audience.

Identifying Audience Needs: To create successful digital products, creators must understand the needs, preferences, and pain points of their audience within their niche. Conducting market research, engaging with their audience through surveys, polls, or comments, and analysing audience feedback and trends can provide valuable insights into the types of digital products that are in demand and resonate with their audience.

Developing High-Quality Content: Developing high-quality content is essential to creating digital products that provide value and resonate with the audience. Creators should leverage their expertise and creativity to develop content that is informative, engaging, and actionable, catering to the specific needs and interests of their audience. Investing time and effort into content creation, design, and presentation can enhance the perceived value of the digital product and increase its appeal to potential buyers.

Setting Pricing and Distribution Strategies: Setting pricing and distribution strategies involves determining the cost of the digital product and deciding how it will be made available to the audience. Creators can adopt various pricing models, such as one-time purchases, subscription-based access, or tiered pricing with different levels of access or benefits. Additionally, creators can choose distribution platforms such as their own website, third-party marketplaces, or online learning platforms to sell and distribute their digital products.

Marketing and Promotion: Marketing and promotion are crucial to driving awareness and sales of digital products to the target audience. Creators can promote their digital products through various channels, including their YouTube channel, website, social media platforms, email newsletters, collaborations with other creators or influencers, and paid advertising campaigns. Offering limited-time promotions, discounts, or bonuses can incentivise purchases and encourage potential buyers to take action.

Providing Customer Support and Feedback: Providing customer support and feedback is essential to maintaining customer satisfaction and fostering long-term relationships with buyers. Creators should offer responsive and helpful customer support to address any questions, concerns, or issues that arise from purchasing or using the digital product. Additionally, soliciting feedback from customers can provide valuable insights for improving the product and future iterations.

Evaluating Performance and Iterating: Evaluating the performance of digital products involves tracking key metrics such as sales, revenue, conversion rates, customer satisfaction, and engagement. Analysing this data allows creators to assess the effectiveness of their product offerings and marketing strategies and make informed decisions to optimise performance. Iterating on the product based on customer feedback and market trends can enhance its value and appeal to the audience over time.

Conclusion: Selling digital products offers YouTube creators a powerful opportunity to monetise their expertise and provide value to their audience beyond traditional advertising revenue. By creating high-quality digital products that cater to the specific needs and interests of their audience, setting effective pricing and distribution strategies, implementing marketing and promotion efforts, and providing excellent customer support and feedback, creators can build a sustainable income stream while enriching their relationship with their audience. With creativity, dedication, and a focus on delivering value, creators can leverage digital products to achieve their goals and establish long-term success in their niche.

Part 14

Content and Endorsements on YouTube

Brand Partnerships represent a significant avenue for YouTube creators to collaborate with established brands, creating sponsored content, brand integrations, or endorsements within their videos. These collaborations offer creators the opportunity to monetise their content, expand their reach, and establish credibility by associating with reputable brands. Understanding the dynamics of brand partnerships and implementing effective strategies can empower creators to cultivate meaningful collaborations that benefit both parties while delivering value to their audience.

Types of Brand Collaborations: Brand collaborations encompass a variety of partnerships, including sponsored content, brand integrations, product placements, endorsements, or ambassadorships. Creators can collaborate with brands across diverse industries and niches, aligning with products, services, or values that resonate with their audience and content.

Creating Sponsored Content: Sponsored content involves creators partnering with brands to feature their products or services in their videos in exchange for compensation. Creators can integrate brand messaging, demonstrations, testimonials, or promotions seamlessly into their content, ensuring relevance and authenticity to their audience while meeting the objectives of the brand.

Implementing Brand Integrations: Brand integrations entail incorporating a brand's products or messaging organically into the creator's video content, enhancing the viewer experience without disrupting the flow or authenticity of the content. Creators can integrate products into tutorials, reviews, vlogs, or storytelling segments, aligning with the context and theme of the video to create a natural and engaging brand experience.

Providing Genuine Endorsements: Genuine endorsements involve creators authentically endorsing or recommending a brand's products or services based on their personal experience, expertise, or affinity. Creators can leverage their credibility and influence to advocate for brands they genuinely believe in, building trust and credibility with their audience while delivering value to the brand.

Negotiating Terms and Compensation: Negotiating terms and compensation involves establishing mutually beneficial agreements between creators and brands, outlining the scope of the collaboration, deliverables, timeline, and compensation. Creators should consider factors such as audience demographics, reach, engagement, content quality, and exclusivity when negotiating terms to ensure fair compensation and alignment with their values and objectives.

Maintaining Authenticity and Transparency:
Maintaining authenticity and transparency is crucial to preserving the trust and credibility of creators with their audience when collaborating with brands. Creators should disclose sponsored content clearly and transparently to their audience, adhering to advertising regulations and guidelines, such as the Federal Trade Commission (FTC) guidelines in the United States, and ensuring that their endorsements are genuine and aligned with their values and principles.

Building Long-Term Relationships: Building long-term relationships with brands involves nurturing ongoing collaborations and partnerships that extend beyond individual campaigns or activations. Creators can demonstrate reliability, professionalism, and value to brands through consistent performance, positive results, and effective communication, fostering trust and loyalty that leads to repeat business and sustained partnerships.

Measuring Impact and Performance: Measuring the impact and performance of brand collaborations involves evaluating key metrics such as reach, engagement, brand sentiment, sales, and return on investment (ROI). Creators can leverage analytics tools, audience feedback, and performance data to assess the effectiveness of their collaborations and make informed decisions to optimize future partnerships.

Conclusion: Brand Partnerships offer YouTube creators valuable opportunities to collaborate with established brands, creating sponsored content, brand integrations, or endorsements that benefit both parties and deliver value to their audience. By fostering authentic, transparent, and mutually beneficial relationships with brands, creators can monetise their content, expand their reach, and enhance their credibility while delivering meaningful experiences to their audience. With creativity, professionalism, and a focus on delivering value, creators can leverage brand partnerships to achieve their goals and establish long-term success on YouTube.

Part 15

Unlocking Revenue Streams: Maximising Opportunities through Licensing Your Content for Media Outlets and Productions

Licensing Your Content provides YouTube creators with a valuable opportunity to monetise their videos by granting permission to media outlets, production companies, or other creators to use their content in various projects in exchange for a licensing fee. This approach allows creators to leverage their content beyond their own platforms, reaching wider audiences and generating additional revenue streams. Understanding the dynamics of content licensing and implementing effective strategies can empower creators to capitalize on this opportunity while protecting their intellectual property rights and maintaining control over their content.

Understanding Content Licensing: Content licensing involves granting permission to third parties to use your videos in their projects, such as news broadcasts, documentaries, advertisements, films, or online content, in exchange for a licensing fee. Creators retain ownership of their content while granting specific rights to the licensee, such as the right to reproduce, distribute, display, or modify the content within the terms of the licensing agreement.

Identifying Licensing Opportunities: Identifying licensing opportunities involves recognising the potential value of your content to media outlets, production companies, or other creators seeking high-quality, relevant footage for their projects. Creators can capitalize on trending topics, viral videos, niche expertise, or unique perspectives within their content to attract potential licensees interested in using their videos for various purposes.

Negotiating Licensing Agreements: Negotiating licensing agreements requires establishing clear terms and conditions that govern the use of your content by the licensee. Creators should specify factors such as the duration of the license, territorial rights, permitted uses, exclusivity, attribution requirements, and compensation terms, ensuring that the agreement protects their rights and interests while providing value to the licensee.

Determining Licensing Fees: Determining licensing fees involves assessing the value of your content based on factors such as the quality, uniqueness, relevance, and demand for the content, as well as the scope and scale of the intended use by the licensee. Creators can establish pricing structures based on factors such as per-minute rates, usage tiers, or flat fees, tailored to the specific needs and budget of the licensee.

Protecting Intellectual Property Rights: Protecting intellectual property rights is paramount when licensing your content to third parties to prevent unauthorised use, infringement, or exploitation of your work. Creators should clearly define the rights granted to the licensee in the licensing agreement and include provisions for enforcing copyright protection, monitoring usage, and addressing any breaches or violations of the agreement.

Promoting Content Licensing Opportunities: Promoting content licensing opportunities involves raising awareness of your content and its availability for licensing to potential licensees. Creators can showcase their portfolio of licensed content on their website, social media platforms, or licensing marketplaces, highlighting the quality, relevance, and versatility of their videos to attract potential buyers.

Managing Licensing Relationships: Managing licensing relationships requires maintaining communication, transparency, and professionalism with licensees throughout the duration of the licensing agreement. Creators should provide prompt responses to inquiries, facilitate the licensing process efficiently, and ensure compliance with the terms of the agreement to foster positive relationships and encourage repeat business.

Evaluating Licensing Performance: Evaluating the performance of content licensing involves monitoring key metrics such as revenue generated, number of licenses sold, types of projects using your content, and feedback from licensees. Creators can use this data to assess the effectiveness of their licensing efforts, identify trends and opportunities, and make informed decisions to optimize their licensing strategy.

Conclusion: Licensing Your Content offers YouTube creators a valuable opportunity to monetise their videos and reach new audiences by granting permission for third parties to use their content in various projects. By understanding the dynamics of content licensing, negotiating agreements, determining fair pricing, protecting intellectual property rights, promoting licensing opportunities, managing relationships with licensees, and evaluating performance, creators can maximize the potential of content licensing as a revenue stream while maintaining control over their content and expanding their reach beyond their own platforms. With strategic planning, professionalism, and a focus on providing value, creators can leverage content licensing to unlock new revenue streams and opportunities for growth in the digital landscape.